Remembering
Cmdr. Michael Smith
Challenger Pilot
USNA class of 1967

HIGH FLIGHT

Oh, I have slipped the surly bonds of earth,
And danced the skies on laughter-silvered wings;
Sunward I've climbed and joined the tumbling mirth
Of sun-split clouds—and done a hundred things
You have not dreamed of—wheeled and soared and swung
High in the sunlit silence. Hov'ring there,
I've chased the shouting wind along and flung
My eager craft through footless halls of air.
Up, up the long, delirious, burning blue
I've topped the wind-swept heights with easy grace,
Where never lark, or even eagle, flew;
And while with silent, lifting mind I've trod
The high, untrespassed sanctity of space,
Put out my hand, and touched the face of God.

—John Gillespie Magee, Jr.,
nineteen-year-old Canadian Air
Force pilot, killed in action in 1941

Cornerstones of Freedom

The Story of

THE CHALLENGER DISASTER

By Zachary Kent

Cover Illustration by Ralph Canaday

CHILDRENS PRESS ®

CHICAGO

Christa McAuliffe at the White House, when she was chosen to travel aboard *Challenger*

Library of Congress Cataloging-in-Publication Data

Kent, Zachary.
    The story of the Challenger disaster.

    (Cornerstones of freedom)
    Summary: An account of the worst disaster in the
twenty-five-year history of United States space
exploration, the loss of the shuttlecraft Challenger
and its seven member crew.
    1. Astronautics—United States—Accidents—1986—
Juvenile literature. 2. Challenger (Spacecraft)—
Juvenile literature. [1. Astronautics—United States—
Accidents—1986. 2. Challenger (Spacecraft)]
I. Canaday, Ralph., ill. II. Title. III. Series.
TL867.K46 1986   363.1'24   86-6822
ISBN 0-516-04673-X

Concord high school students watching *Challenger* blast off

In Concord, New Hampshire, people arose with a feeling of high expectation. It was January 28, 1986, and the space shuttle *Challenger* was scheduled to blast into orbit that day. Traveling on the spacecraft was a Concord schoolteacher named Christa McAuliffe. Although American military pilots, scientists, and even politicians had shuttled into space before, McAuliffe would be the first private citizen in the United States to make the thrilling flight.

Late in the morning excited students filled the Concord High School auditorium to witness the shuttle launch on television. Many showed their festive mood by wearing party hats and blowing noisemakers. Newsmen and camera crews lined the

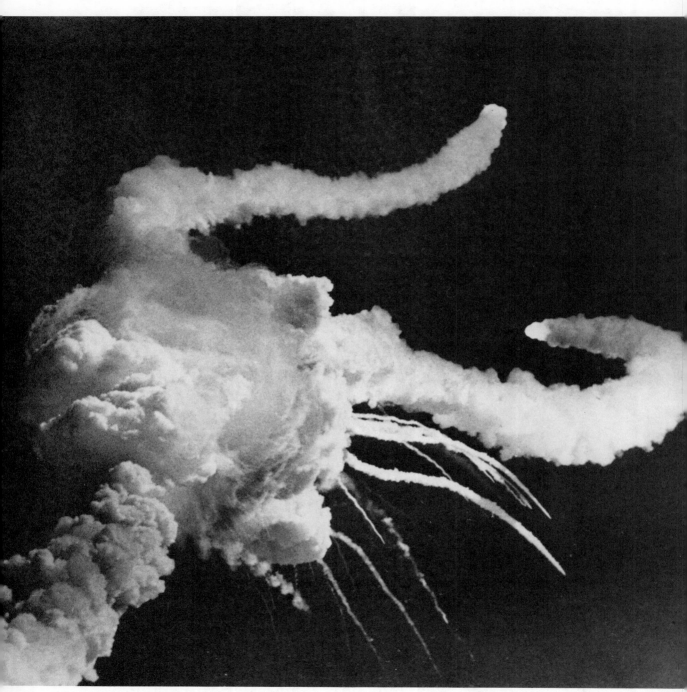

Challenger explodes shortly after lift-off.

walls to record the happy scene. Watching the television screen, the students loudly joined in, calling out the final countdown. "... Three ... two ... one ... lift-off!" they shouted as the rockets boosted the shuttle from the launchpad. Sudden cheers and clapping rang throughout the room. Students unfurled a banner that read, "We're with U Christa." The noise continued as the *Challenger* arched up through the air, leaving a thick trail of smoke behind it. With pride and wonder these young people watched their teacher speed toward space.

In another moment an unexpected flash burst across the screen. "Shut up, everyone!" yelled a teacher who realized something was wrong. The auditorium fell into silence as a television voice announced, "The vehicle has exploded." Young faces stared in disbelief as smiles turned to tears. No one ever dreamed that such a horrible thing could happen. Later, in grief, Principal Charles Foley told reporters, "We were enjoying the entire event. We were celebrating with her. Then it stopped. That's all. ... It just stopped."

As the tragedy sank in, weeping students and teachers returned to their classrooms. Within an hour Principal Foley sent everyone home. Outside

Christa McAuliffe's sister Lisa and parents, Grace and Ed Corrigan, watch as the shuttle explodes.

the school, a reporter approached one student, Rusty Spalding, for his reaction to the explosion. "Shocked, very shocked," the young man revealed with tears in his eyes. "I felt as if my whole body blew up inside when I saw that. And I can just never be as shocked as I am now."

That afternoon millions of people across the nation shared in those sad feelings. In a stunning instant, a time of joy and triumph turned into a nightmare. In its twenty-five years of space exploration, the United States had never suffered a worse disaster than the loss of the shuttlecraft *Challenger* and its seven-member crew.

America's earliest astronauts well understood the dangers of flying into space. Veteran astronaut

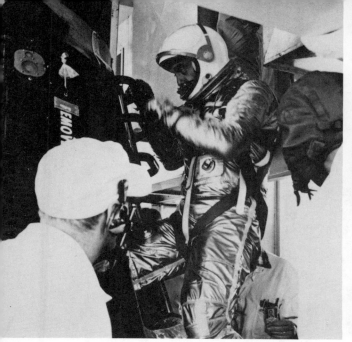

Astronauts Alan Shepard (left) and Walter Schirra (right)

Walter Schirra, Jr., remarked, "We felt we were flying in the safest machine you could put together. But the potential was always there. . . . It's a risky business."

After Alan B. Shepard, Jr., became the first American in space on May 5, 1961, the program of the National Aeronautics and Space Administration (NASA) advanced without a major misfortune. The successes of the *Mercury* and *Gemini* space flights left America unprepared when tragedy first struck on January 27, 1967. On that day Virgil "Gus" Grissom, Edward H. White, and Roger B. Chaffee trained for the first mission in NASA's Apollo program. The three pilots sat in their space capsule atop a *Saturn* rocket on the Cape Canaveral,

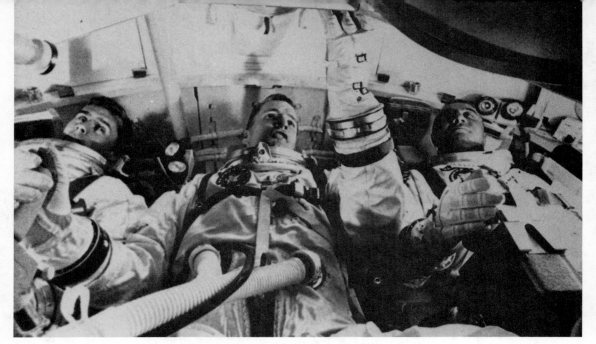

Apollo 1 crew (left to right), Roger Chaffee, Edward White, and Virgil Grissom

Florida, launchpad. Minutes into their training exercise Gus Grissom's frantic voice called mission control. "Fire! We've got a fire in the cockpit!" In another fourteen seconds a second voice, probably Roger Chaffee's, cried, "We've got a bad fire! Let's get out. . . . We're burning up!" Smoke and flames poured from the capsule. By the time technicians could come to their aid, the three astronauts had died of burns and suffocation.

The *Apollo* tragedy, caused when faulty wiring sent sparks into the capsule's pure oxygen air, halted America's space program for over twenty months. When the *Apollo* flights finally continued, they led to *Apollo 11*'s successful landing on the moon on July 20, 1969. "That's one small step for

Left: Neil Armstrong walks on the moon. Right: Moscow memorial to the *Soyuz 11* crew

man, one giant leap for mankind," announced Neil Armstrong as he became the first human to set foot on the moon. In that wonderful moment Americans regained their confidence in NASA's projects.

Americans were not the only ones to risk their lives while exploring space. In the history of its space program the Soviet Union suffered two tragic accidents. On April 24, 1967, the *Soyuz 1* space capsule crashed on reentry. Its parachute failed to open and cosmonaut Vladimir Komarov died. Then on June 29, 1971, cosmonauts Georgi Dobrovolsky, Vladislav Volkov, and Viktor Patsayev met sudden death during the reentry of *Soyuz 11*. The returning capsule lost pressure due to a faulty seal, and the three brave men suffocated.

Undaunted, NASA believed it could solve whatever problems the American space program encountered. NASA readied itself for the next big step in space exploration. In 1972 President Richard Nixon authorized the development of the space shuttle. During the next nine years scientists and engineers created a spacecraft that allowed orbiting astronauts to return to Earth by landing like an airplane on an airstrip. This reusable, thick-bodied "shuttle" measured 120 feet long from nose to tail and 80 feet across its delta-shaped wings. When the space shuttle *Columbia* first blasted into orbit on April 12, 1981, piloted by John Young and Robert Crippen, it marked the start of a bold new era in space flight. The shuttle proved its worth in successive flights by launching communications satellites from its 60- by 15-foot cargo bay. Its scientific equipment conducted valuable ecological and industrial experiments such as mapping Earth's flood and air pollution areas and mixing chemical elements in the zero gravity of space.

On April 4, 1983, NASA successfully launched its second shuttle, *Challenger*. More streamlined than the *Columbia, Challenger* soon proved itself the workhorse of the shuttles. Though the *Discovery*

Above: *Challenger* in 1983
Right: Sally Ride and Guion Bluford

and the *Atlantis* later joined the fleet, time after time NASA returned to use *Challenger*. Landing again and again at Edwards Air Force Base in California, *Challenger* presented a glorious sight. On its second trip on June 18, 1983, *Challenger* carried America's first woman into space, Sally Ride. Guion Bluford, the country's first black astronaut, flew with the crew on *Challenger*'s third mission.

In the summer of 1984 President Ronald Reagan announced that the first person in the nation's Space Flight Participant Program would be a teacher. In a flurry of excitement more than eleven thousand American educators applied for the position. Giving each application careful consideration, NASA narrowed its choices to ten finalists. On July 19, 1985, at a White House ceremony Vice-President George Bush named thirty-six-year-old Christa McAuliffe to be the "first private citizen passenger in the history of space flight." Overcome by her selection McAuliffe thanked him saying, "It's not often that a teacher is at a loss for words."

Overnight all of America wanted to learn about the lucky social studies teacher and follow her activities. One NASA official told reporters, "Her enthusiasm is a very infectious thing. She's a natural for the mission." Her friends and pupils agreed. "She's the kind of person who could come back and relate it meaningfully to her students," revealed Concord High School Principal Foley. In her application McAuliffe had stated her desire to keep a flight journal that would "humanize the technology of the Space Age" for students. She believed her experiences as a pioneer space traveler might

The McAuliffes: Scott, Steven, Caroline, and Christa

one day be compared with those of the pioneers who journeyed West in Conestoga wagons. "I really hope the students get excited about the Space Age because they see me as an ordinary person up there in space," she told an interviewer.

On her return home to Concord, the town welcomed McAuliffe with a parade. Newspapers throughout New Hampshire ran feature stories about her. Camera crews visited the modest house where she lived with her lawyer husband, Steven, and their two children. Through it all McAuliffe remained enthusiastic. "I just can't believe people are so excited and proud," she cheerfully exclaimed.

At last the time arrived for McAuliffe to begin her training at the Johnson Space Center in Houston, Texas. Saying good-bye to her children was difficult.

"I don't want her to go in space, because I just want her to stay around my house," five-year-old Caroline had said. "See ya later, alligator," Christa McAuliffe lovingly called to her daughter as she left for the airport. Within her baggage was a stuffed toy frog named Fleegle, which she had promised her nine-year-old son Scott she would carry into space for him.

At the Johnson Space Center NASA workers prepared McAuliffe for her *Challenger* mission. Day after day she studied training manuals to learn about life in orbit. She read about procedures for dealing with space accidents and about emergency landings. Wearing NASA's bright blue flight suit, she experienced weightlessness in a space agency training jet and spent many other hours aloft. At meals she sometimes ate specially packaged foods just as she would in space. She also spent time becoming friends with her fellow crew members.

The six people joining Christa McAuliffe on *Challenger*'s tenth voyage into space were skilled

Challenger commander
Francis R. Scobee

pilots and knowledgeable scientists representing a cross section of America. The commander of the mission, forty-six-year-old Francis "Dick" Scobee, had flown in *Challenger* once before. The crew during that 1984 trip repaired a solar satellite in space. Born in Cle Elum, Washington, Scobee rose through the ranks of the Air Force. As a pilot he logged more than 6,500 hours of flight time in forty-five types of aircraft. Before joining the astronaut program in 1978 Scobee piloted the Boeing 747 jet that carried the test shuttle *Enterprise* "piggyback" between landing and launching areas.

Challenger pilot Michael J. Smith

Navy Commander Michael J. Smith was a seasoned flier also, but he had never been in space before. The forty-year-old from Beaufort, North Carolina, gladly jumped at the chance to become part of the *Challenger* crew. A United States Naval Academy graduate, Smith flew A-6 Intruder jets from the deck of the aircraft carrier *Kitty Hawk* during the Vietnam War. For his combat services he received a number of high military honors. After five years in the astronaut program, NASA finally chose Smith to pilot the *Challenger*.

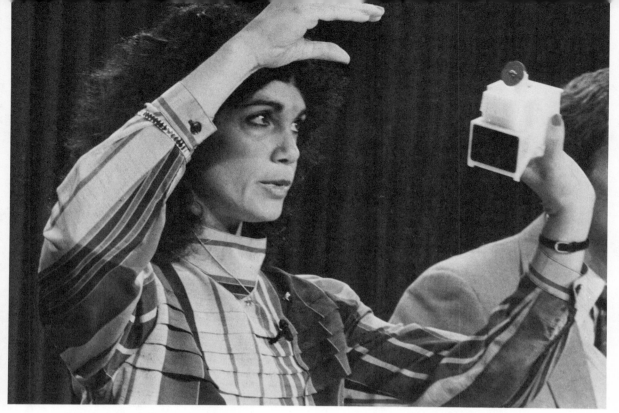

Mission specialist Judith A. Resnik

Thirty-six-year-old Dr. Judith A. Resnik was a space travel veteran. In 1984 she became the second American woman in space and the first Jewish astronaut. As the shuttle *Discovery* first entered orbit, an enthusiastic Resnik radioed back, "The Earth looks great!" When ice formed on the shuttle's side, Resnik used the craft's long robot arm to break a chunk off. With the rest of the *Discovery* crew, Resnik logged 144 hours and 57 minutes in space. NASA picked the Akron, Ohio, native—trained as an electrical engineer—to be one of the three mission specialists on the *Challenger* flight.

Mission specialist Ronald E. McNair and his wife, Cheryl

Another mission specialist was thirty-five-year-old Dr. Ronald E. McNair. When this expert laser physicist traveled into orbit in 1984, he became America's second black to travel in space. Growing up in Lake City, South Carolina, during the difficult 1950s and 1960s, McNair learned not to let racial prejudice stand in the way of his goals. It meant "trying a little harder, fighting a little harder to get what you perhaps deserve," he remembered. With an advanced degree from the Massachusetts Institute of Technology, McNair joined the astronaut program in 1978. While aboard *Challenger*, orbiting

Mission specialist Ellison S. Onizuka

in space, McNair was to launch a small science platform to study Halley's comet.

Air Force Lieutenant Colonel Ellison S. Onizuka first journeyed aloft in January 1985 when the shuttle *Discovery* made a secret military flight. Now NASA chose him to be *Challenger*'s third mission specialist. As a boy in Kealakekua, Kona, Hawaii, the thirty-nine-year-old aerospace engineer dreamed of becoming a space explorer. For the *Challenger* voyage, this Japanese-American explained, "I'll be looking at Halley's comet. . . . They tell me I'll have one of the best views around."

Left to right: Payload specialist Gregory B. Jarvis, Florida Congressman Bill Nelson, and Utah Senator Jake Garn

Perhaps the most eager crew member was payload specialist Gregory B. Jarvis. Scheduled for two earlier crews, Jarvis had lost his place first to Utah Senator Jake Garn. The first congressman in space, Garn flew on the *Discovery* in April 1985. Later NASA bumped Jarvis again to allow Florida congressman Bill Nelson to shuttle on the most recent trip of the *Columbia*. Finally it seemed the Hughes Aircraft Company engineer would get his chance to fly with the *Challenger* crew. The forty-one-year-old from Mohawk, New York, planned to spend six days in orbit studying weightless liquids and figuring out better ways to build satellites.

NASA assigned Christa McAuliffe additional duties also. While in space the teacher would broadcast two live lessons on television to the nation's schoolchildren. The first would explain the roles of the crew, and the second, the purpose of space exploration. As the launch date neared, a reporter asked if McAuliffe felt fearful. "Not yet," she answered. "Maybe when I'm strapped in and those rockets are going off underneath me I will be, but space flight today really seems safe."

At last the *Challenger* crew flew to Cape Canaveral in preparation for the January 25, 1986, lift-off date. Anxiously they waited for acceptable weather conditions.

On that Saturday NASA postponed the flight because of poor conditions at emergency landing strips in Africa. On Sunday officials scratched a second attempt because Florida forecasts looked bad. On Monday high winds made trying to launch unsafe. After waiting five hours while strapped on their backs in shuttle seats, the seven crew members learned of their third delay.

Finally, Tuesday, January 28, 1986, dawned clear and cold in Florida. Although icicles formed on the upended shuttle, NASA officials seemed confident.

Challenger crew members leaving their quarters to board the shuttle on the morning of January 28, 1986. Left to right: Ellison Onizuka, Gregory Jarvis, Christa McAuliffe, Michael Smith

"Let's go today," a smiling Christa McAuliffe called to reporters as the astronauts left for the launch tower. While they suited up to enter the shuttle, a cheerful NASA technician presented an apple to the teacher for good luck. After two hours of delays, the launch seemed ready for countdown at 11:38 A.M.

On the ground thousands of people with binoculars and cameras prepared to watch *Challenger* roar into space. Close friends and relatives of the crew members stood on bleachers gazing at the magnificent shuttle. Eighteen third-grade classmates of Scott McAuliffe waved a banner that read, "Go Christa." From loudspeakers everyone heard the voice of mission control and the public affairs officer.

Space Shuttle Explodes
10.35 miles high - 8.05 miles downrange from launching pad

THE LAST SECONDS

Mission Commentator: 10-9-8-7-6, we have main engine start, 4-3-2-1, and liftoff. Liftoff of the 25th space shuttle mission. And it has cleared the tower.

Pilot Mike Smith: Roll program.

Mission Control: Roger, roll, Challenger.

Mission Control Commentator: Roll program confirmed. Challenger now heading down range. The engines are throttling down now at 94 percent. Normal throttle for most of the flight is 104 percent. We'll throttle down to 65 percent shortly. Engines at 65 percent. Three engines running normally. Three good fuel cells. Three good APUs (auxiliary power units). Velocity 2257 feet per second (1400 miles per hour), altitude 4.3 nautical miles (4.9 statute miles), downrange distance 3 nautical miles (3.4 statute miles). Engines throttling up, three engines now 104 percent.

Mission Control: Challenger, go at throttle up.

Smith: Roger, go at throttle up. (Fireball occurs)

Mission Control Commentator: We're at a minute 15 seconds, velocity 2900 feet per second (1977 mph) altitude 9 nautical miles (10.35 statute miles), range distance 7 nautical miles (8.05 statute miles)

There was a long silence.

Mission Control Commentator: Flight controllers are looking very carefully at the situation. Obviously a major malfunction. We have no downlink (communications).

"T minus 10, 9, 8, 7, 6, we have main engine start, 4, 3, 2, 1. And lift-off. Lift-off of the twenty-fifth space shuttle mission, and it has cleared the tower."

Its engines blazing, *Challenger* thrust quickly up and away. Its rockets trailing clouds of smoke, the shuttle picked up speed.

"Velocity 2,257 feet per second," the loudspeaker announced. Witnesses strained their eyes to watch the spacecraft's progress.

"*Challenger,* go with throttle up," instructed mission control. "Roger, go with throttle up," answered Commander Scobee's voice.

Then, seventy-four seconds after the shuttle left the ground, the sky suddenly lit up with a stunning white-orange fireball. People stared in confusion as the left and right rocket boosters crazily spun away from the explosion.

"Flight controllers here looking very carefully at the situation," informed the public affairs officer. Then after a long pause he solemnly continued, "We have a report . . . that the vehicle has exploded."

Comrades and loved ones shook with grief on the viewing stand. After fifty million miles of shuttle travel without an accident, the worst possible disaster had just occurred before their eyes. Many still could not believe it. Some kept staring hopefully. Some openly sobbed and hugged one another. Slowly they walked away.

Seven miles west of Cape Canaveral a Coast Guard cutter gently rocked in the water. The *Point Roberts* with its ten-man crew remained stationed below *Challenger*'s flight path. Stunned crewmen watched small fragments of the shuttle rain down into the ocean for an hour. "We were awestruck," explained Lieutenant John Philbin. Soon NASA directed the *Point Roberts* to gather whatever wreckage it could find. Other boats and planes promptly joined the search, but little hope remained that any of the seven crew members survived.

Whatever the reason for the tragedy, the nation

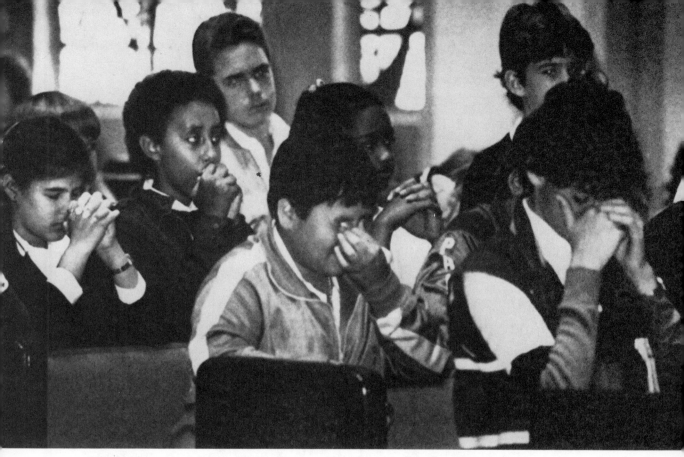

Schoolchildren in Orlando, Florida, at a memorial service for the shuttle crew

mourned its loss as the news spread. Across the country church bells tolled and citizens lowered flags to half-staff. In Washington, D.C., the chaplain of the House of Representatives offered up a prayer. From the floor of the House, Congresswoman Lynn Martin honored the fallen seven.

"Now their names become history. But that drive of the human spirit will not die," she reminded her listeners. "In that flash and fire it will be reborn again in other young men and young women who will read about them and learn."

Other American leaders also stepped forward to offer sympathy. Former astronaut Senator John Glenn mourned, "This is a day we've managed to avoid for a quarter of a century. . . . It finally has arrived. We'd hoped we could push this day back forever."

With tears in his eyes, Senator Garn spoke of confidence in the space program. "I would go again tomorrow. If NASA would let me go, I would go again."

Flying to Cape Canaveral, Vice-President Bush met with the crew members' grieving families. Afterwards he remarked, "We must never, as people in our daily lives or as a nation, stop exploring, stop hoping, stop discovering. We must press on."

Word of the shuttle disaster greatly affected President Reagan. Canceling plans to make his annual State of the Union Address that night, he addressed the nation that afternoon instead. In a televised speech from the Oval Office the president declared, "We mourn seven heroes. . . . We mourn their loss as a nation together.

"The families of the seven—we cannot bear, as you do, the full impact of this tragedy, but we feel the loss and we're thinking about you so very much.

Your loved ones . . . had that special spirit that says, 'Give me a challenge and I'll meet it with joy.' They had a hunger to explore the universe and discover its truths. They wished to serve and they did—they served us all."

To America's schoolchildren he explained, "I know it's hard to understand that sometimes painful things like this happen. It's all part of the process of exploration and discovery; it's all part of taking a chance and expanding man's horizons. The future doesn't belong to the fainthearted. It belongs to the brave. . . . The crew of the space shuttle *Challenger* honored us by the manner in which they lived their lives. We will never forget them nor the last time we saw them this morning as they prepared for their journey and waved good-bye and 'slipped the surly bonds of earth to touch the face of God.' "

Three days after the tragedy, governors, congressmen, foreign diplomats, and NASA engineers and technicians gathered in Houston. More than fifteen thousand people crowded the lawn of the Johnson Space Center for a national memorial service. An Air Force band quietly played patriotic tunes. Then President Reagan stepped before this audience to speak again.

"What we say today is only an inadequate expression of what we carry in our hearts," he said. "Words pale in the shadow of grief. . . . The best we can do is remember our seven astronauts—our *Challenger* Seven. . . . We remember Dick Scobee . . . Michael Smith . . . Judith Resnik . . . Ellison Onizuka . . . Ronald McNair . . . Gregory Jarvis. . . . We remember Christa McAuliffe, who captured the imagination of the entire nation."

Addressing their parents, wives, and children, he continued, "The sacrifice of your loved ones has stirred the soul of our nation and, through the pain, our hearts have been opened to a profound truth: the future is not free, the story of all human progress is one of a struggle against all odds. . . . Our seven star voyagers . . . answered a call beyond duty."

With words of hope the president promised, "Man will continue his conquest of space, to reach out for new goals and ever greater achievements. That is the way we shall commemorate our seven *Challenger* heroes."

After the president returned to his seat, four roaring T38 jets streaked overhead through the sky. Beneath gray clouds they flew in the "Missing Man" formation, a final tribute to the *Challenger* crew.

Front row: Michael J. Smith, Francis R. Scobee, Ronald E. McNair
Back row: Ellison S. Onizuka, Sharon Christa McAuliffe, Gregory B. Jarvis, Judith A. Resnik

In Concord, New Hampshire, during the days that followed, Mrs. Virginia Timmons finally took down from her front window the note Christa McAuliffe had once written to her daughter, Jeanne. "May your future be limited only by your dreams. Love, Christa," it read.

Life slowly returned to normal in Concord and throughout the nation, but never will we forget our teacher, Christa McAuliffe, who encouraged us all to "reach for the stars."

About the Author

Zachary Kent grew up in the town of Little Falls, New Jersey. He is a graduate of St. Lawrence University and holds a teaching certificate in English. Following college he was employed at a New York City literary agency for two years until he decided to launch a career as a writer. To support himself while writing, he has worked as a taxi driver, a shipping clerk, and a house painter.

Mr. Kent has had a lifelong interest in American history. As a boy the study of the United States presidents was his special hobby. His collection of presidential items includes books, pictures, and games, as well as several autographed letters.

Joining all of America in mourning its tragic loss, Mr. Kent hopes this book does some justice to the memories of *Challenger*'s fallen heroes.

About the Artist

Ralph Canaday has been involved in all aspects of commercial art since graduation from the Art Institute of Chicago in 1959. He is an illustrator, designer, painter, and sculptor whose work has appeared in many national publications, textbooks, and corporate promotional materials. Mr. Canaday lives in Hanover Park, Illinois, with his wife Arlene, who is also in publishing.

Photo Credits

AP/Wide World Photos—4, 5, 6, 8, 10, 15, 17, 18, 19, 21, 22 (center and right), 24, 25, 27, 31

Courtesy National Aeronautics and Space Administration—2, 9 (left), 11 (left), 13 (3 photos)

UPI/Bettmann Newsphotos—9 (right), 11 (right), 20, 22 (left)